MAY MAGIC MOMENTS FIND YOU

POETRY FOR FELLOW WANDERERS

K.L. LOVELACE

for
my ancestors
of the past, present and future
and for everyone
trying their best
to lead with love
through the ups and downs,
the cycles of time

thank you for reading

contents

A note from the author: on magic & poetry

The way that these short poems flowed through me felt like magic. Teaching me that magic is all around us, if only we are ready to receive it. Magic is receptivity to universal messages, and it is also what you do with it. It is living with an openness to receive and an intentionality to engage.

I am no expert, and only just dipping my toes into vast sources of magic, esotericism and history. But you do not have to be an expert to let your intuition guide you. These histories are within us, after all.

My first magical crush, as many before me, is on the gorgeous and knowing moon. The promise of a certain rhythm that carries us ever-forward as we ebb and flow with luminosity and darkness. I find this rhythm both divine and reassuring. I love that while the moon is always moving forward, she is also always retracing her orbital steps, gathering ever more insight in order to develop a fuller picture as time marches on.

I've organized these poems to align with the cycle of the moon. This is more about the moon's path than it is the exact phases; each section representing a leg of the journey.

The truth is that every part of the cycle contains multitudes, as cycles are infinite and layered. I hope that in these pages you find affirmations, reflections and releases that are meaningful to you on your journey, fellow traveler.

Self understanding

In this place we discover ourselves. In this part of the cycle the moon is new; dark in the sky, reflecting no light.

What feels true about yourself right now, in your soul and in your body? Where are you standing within the metaverse?

Is this place new to you, or is it something you keep coming back to? Both can be true. We start new cycles and carry old ones at the same time; linearity is a fallacy.

Meeting myself

i looked in the mirror
and saw myself
freckles, zits, scars
pink skin
dark eyes
dive in

Snapping crab

i am defensive
been defending
my whole life

my right to be me
be loved
love my hobbies
feel my feelings

...

i can shed my defense

it never served me well
hurting myself
with my own weapons

Pandemic or not

stayed home alone
for a whole year
and I still love

mascara
lip gloss
a good hair day
feeling cute
dressing up

confirmation

that it was always
for me

Sagittarius lifestyle

i trust, letting faith lead
following a dream, feet stumbling

people don't like getting bumped into
by someone with their head in the clouds

come back down
keep a full heart but look around

don't go too fast, accept redirection
listen; the universe speaks

dreams may be ahead or slip
back and around

this body knows today, root down

history
billions of years old
it's not a language with words I know

but I know truth, reverence, connectedness

Mercurial mind

the calculations
always sifting through my mind
freaky
powerful
vulnerable
a rabbit hole

No limits

i have been eaten alive
by the fantasy
of one true love

not the truth, the narrative

i have dutifully longed for it
my whole life

but do I even believe in love
so limited?

my story includes the potential for
ever-lasting love

but also...

here i am
unwinding
what love is

making space for

Love and loss
Platonic love
Familial love
Romantic love
Love of my body
Fleeting love
Love of food
Love for animals
Love for Earth
Love that lasts one encounter, or three
Love that doesn't change hard circumstances
Practical love
Careful love
Love of craft
Love of deep feeling
Love of love

Visions

out ahead of things
sometimes even myself

Dreaming of now

slow down
breathe
let time sit inside you

the fullness of each moment

don't rush to anything
nowhere is more important
than where you are

time is moving with you
not against you

in this moment there is space to dream
what is it you dream of?

Ageless soul

my body is new
to this practice
to this world
but my soul is old

Self centered

not everything
is about you

but your life is about you
don't forget that

My voice

i have a voice
that can be heard
i will try to use it well

sometimes I'm loud
told to quiet down
i don't really know how

my tongue can bite
unknowingly curt
people want honesty
only when it doesn't hurt

i try to learn
the art of delivery
never been accused
of inauthenticity

i have a voice
that can be heard
i will try to use it well

Intentions

when your intentions are pure
you don't mind
when they are questioned
the answer is easy

being understood
is not your burden

You think, and so do I

every thought you have
is from your own perspective

The way we are

it seems in times of tension
we shut off
shut off to pain
shut off to responsibility

and shut off to possibility

it's not making us stronger

we are in a drain
racing down the whirlpool
of fear

let love in
i love you

Initiating action

Here we take our first shaky steps into the world. As the moon moves past it's new phase and toward the first quarter, she is in new territory; a little shaky on her feet but brave in the face of turbulence. She has just been reminded of her core, and with that fire inside her she steps into the headwinds.

In the first leg of the journey we were getting to know ourselves and understanding our starting place. Here we begin to assert ourselves, we take action within our environment. We are met with initial blocks, from within our own minds or from the external world and we still choose to move forward.

No reason

create
for the sake of it

Mental blocks

an epiphany
that some of my mental blocks
are unnecessary

like.. who says?

Uniquely you

find yourself
and be that

Love unbounded

my love has been discounted

by family
friends
lovers
myself

my love is rich
it is deep
unbounded

Reverberations

i'm broken
from things
i can't even remember

Fear

i fear

i will never be chosen
i will die alone
i don't know what I want
commitment to place
i'll never be financially stable
i am unloved
i am unlovable

A mindset

there is enough

shedding the illusion of lack
living in abundance

for myself
and for the world

Deep thoughts

feelings can
and sometimes should
be amended

facts can not

science will always be amended

what makes a fact?

On faith

outside of any god
having faith
is knowing that

moving through life
is, in itself
a valuable experience

On purpose

consider,
the things
that make you feel the most
scared
could be your lessons

Journeyman

insecurities will bring down the ship
root them out in yourself
don't bring them in your carry on

Growth

i am expansive
yet exist in this form

my body does not limit
my imagination
my creation

You are doing it

Here we have hit our stride. As the moon moves between the first quarter and full we gain our confidence. The scariest part of the road is behind us and we are filling our own cup. By doing so, we easily and without hesitation share our spirit with others.

We are interacting with the world and we are fearless in our quest, whatever that may be. It is inspiring to be in this place, and you are inspiring to witness.

She is powerful

i feel an energy in me
it runs in the ground
and in the sky
i feel it in my fingertips
electrifying

she is powerful
she has power
she is me

Subversive strength

i constantly question: is it me?
and sometimes, yes

self awareness
rooted in my femininity

i accept fault
taught not to question authority
a consistent message
the burden of responsibility

i unlearn this every day

but it is because
i can question myself
that i am open

to new ideas
different ways of seeing

a strength
a tool for progress

Asking for help

learning how to ask people for things
starting with myself

Bodyworks

abs
abdominals
you hold my stomach together
but we don't have a good relationship

i don't need you to be
beautiful
hot
fuckable
flat

you help me lengthen my lower back
allow mobility in my body
keep me connected
to the light inside of me

i am unlocking a love for you
a love for me

For me

i'm sorry you're hurting
but I need to be in a relationship
with someone who can love me

That's life

you will never agree with someone else
100% of the time

get comfortable
in your own thoughts and opinions
learn how to disagree

Little joys

it's the little things I can do for myself

i don't have to own a home
or have a partner
to have a tea collection
or to dance

tapping into my joy
now
learning how to access it

Movement

love is all around you
love is a choice
love is a flower
blooming with life

cycling through death
each year re-emerging
to remind you it is eternal

love is inside you
love is outside you

it cannot be contained in only one person
it is beautiful to share with
any one person

love is movement
love is a movement
love moves
move into love

Solar gold

called to the sunset
riches in the sky
riches for humanity
owned by no one

On defining ourselves

being a woman is not
the absence of being a man

how many times
will I have to explain this in my life

A moment of truth

You've climbed the mountain and you have a new perspective. We have reached the full moon phase.

It is a moment of understanding, a jolt of awareness. We started from a place of self-understanding, but then we went into the world and our self was challenged.

Maybe this lookout spot offers you a bit of gentle perspective, perhaps an affirmation of alignment, or maybe it is a rude awakening that the path back to yourself might be a bit rough.

My terms

i am both

not a sex object
and
deliciously sexual

on my own terms

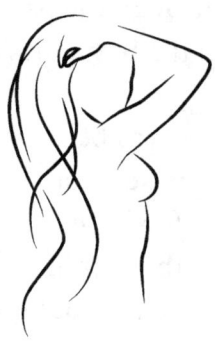

The shove I needed

thank you, and i'm sorry

i learned about me
shadows squirming
uncomfortably near the surface

for years, centuries

i didn't want to look at myself
but I was hiding
from the wrong things

through the pain
i found the best parts of me

whether it was because of you
or in spite of you
you forced me into
the depths
of my soul

i found dark matter and cliff edges
dangerous rapids and demons
traumas buried in my lifetime
and those buried in lifetimes before me

i also found the occasional rainbow
majestic waterfalls
the fruit of life, and spirit

thank you for the push

i hoped that you could hold all of me
rainbows and waterfalls
rapids and cliffs

but it wasn't you

you had me convinced
i was only darkness
with you I stopped seeing my light

i became someone I hated
so that I could become new

On being wrong

we can hold space
for both
being wrong
and
being worthy

Do your best, then let it go

you don't always get to choose
what people see you as

Here in this moment

Black Lives Matter
Black voices lead

i am not an exception
this is soul work
this is life work

listen
think
apply

we can be the change
i will be the change

Huh, a concept

date people who like you
who tell you they like you

i wish this was
as obvious as it sounds

Asking tough questions

what do you consider a livable wage?

what are you willing to live on?

are they different?

why?

Blame

i don't carry a weapon
no matter how many times
it's recommended

not because I won't need it
a small act of opposition

because I should not have
to carry my burden
in my purse

but I know in my defiance
i am the one who may get hurt

stuck between
blame, shame and victimhood
no place to stand

crushed
no matter which way
the tower lands

An awakening

this is not my first
it will not be my last

may it be lasting

Shocking and predictable times

what is treated as
unbelievable
was easy to see coming

are we really surprised?

hate and disconnection
have been spinning and rushing
like rising waters through our landscape
increasing in pace

Please listen

fires
hurricanes
floods

the earth has been talking for years
now she's screaming
we should listen

Tough deal

not everything has a pretty spin

Riding the wave

Now that you've seen the light, how will you carry it? Here we go, as the moon starts losing light between her fullness and the last quarter phase.

You are still the person you were yesterday, but with new information. Nobody expects you to change on a dime, no matter how life-altering your insight. It is helpful to know that in a month we will be back at this moon phase, and in a year we will be back at same place. Five years ago we were here and five years from now we will be here again; even on our forward journey we still circle back.

Maybe you boldly share your new insight, perhaps it's still giving you aftershocks, maybe you're enjoying the dance of braiding it into your being; either way now we're integrating.

Say it with me

i have value
and I don't have to prove it

A prayer for strength

i can hold my emotions tenderly
with an open heart
for those around me
i am protected
through my connection
to my intuition
and the Earth that holds me

Battling the demon

autonomy was the spark
for the American revolution
immediately denied of other humans

that was a choice
we must face that demon

how to face a demon:

kill it
grieve it

how to kill a demon:
acknowledge it, name it

colonialism
white supremacy
racism
patriarchy

it hides in our safe spaces
created by our secrets

family secrets
generations of burying shame
hoping things might just
magically go away

how to grieve a demon:
come with me through the stages

Shock and Denial:
oh my gosh I can't believe it,
it's so sad, a tragedy
crocodile tears

Anger:
wanting to scream at everyone, shutting
yourself off to the world

Bargaining:
over apologizing, distancing yourself from
your privilege
anger at "them", the problem, those you
think not as evolved as you
avoiding your own participation

Depression:
feeling the heaviness of reality, drowning
sorrows with substances, never talking
about it

Acceptance:
white supremacy and violence against the
feminine are at the root of our history
my history, my country, my family
generational gaslighting
sweeping away any accountability

i am not the first of my lineage
to fight this demon
I accept my mission

Let it be so

i am a revolutionary woman

Flow

i am an artist
of many forms
the curves of my pen
echo the curves of nature
the curves of plants
of my hips as they swing in circles

It never stops

review
revise
renew

we are bound to make mistakes
i cannot change my past
i can take time
look back
switch my approach

i will continue to develop
i am new every time I learn

Dance through it

see your feelings
acknowledge your feelings
dance with your feelings
love your feelings

Shit, this is the work

a cleansing cry
after a layer
of white supremacy
bubbled up
and I let it go
these things come outta nowhere
like
BAM everything you know is a lie...

Let it go and begin again

Whether your journey to this place has been rainbow sherbet or rocky road, on we go as the moon sheds all of it's light and all of it's load.

The next step will be to begin again. It's time to shake it off. Release what is burdening you. The lesson is already planted, you can loosen your grip.

How might you prepare for the next seed of growth? Clear out the mental pests and nurture your body and mind to create a fertile environment for a new cycle of growth.

Sorry it sucks

your feelings are real
but you cannot control the outcome

Releasing to receive

i cleanse myself
of limiting beliefs
about my value

i clear myself from past hurts
that made me shrink and believe
that i was not enough

i am worthy of abundance
of love
of wealth
and I open myself to receive it

Asses everywhere

i'm sorry
to the people
i've been an ass to
because i did not love myself

a big fuck off
to the people
who have been an ass to me
because i did not love myself

Transformation

this time is different
let it be so

don't let the year slip away
without considering the ways
you've cracked, you've grown

let it come up, and let it wash away
create a clean space

experiences, feelings, memories

don't stuff it away
because it's not all rosy
don't vow to move on
and never look back

hear the message
things are changing
let it shake your body
release the need to react

you are clearing a path
for who you are becoming

Feeling good

It's good to feel good

rub lotion all over
your soft, sensual skin
like you love yourself

Space for relating

less judgment
less reactions
more holding space
listening
not trying to explain

Pain is not forever

i forgive myself
for things I handled poorly
because i wasn't doing well
disconnected from myself
fractures of me
i don't have to revisit those moments
over and over in my memories

i release them

we've been here before

don't shoot the messenger
the moon
the mother

reminding us where we've been
always excavating   ˙
feelings well burried

dismissal and defense
invalidate her experience

don't shoot the messenger
the moon
the mother

This ride

i bathe in cosmic waters
contained on this vessel

washing
in the expanse of time
swirling
in the sensual pleasures of this moment

surrounded by everything
but safely contained
free to ride the Milky Way

Legacy

my ancestors remind me
that I am not a hero
i am a human

i am an imprint on this moment
and they are an imprint on me
our impact exponential, surviving infinitely

time goes forward
and stretches back

i'm a spec in the cosmos
trying my best